Brain Awakes

Brain Awakes:

Empowering Children Through Breath, Balance, and Reflection

Joseph Hamer and Hayley Peter

Illustration by Allison Stucky

Printed in the United States of America

First Printing, 2020

ISBN-13: 978-1-949001-55-6 print edition
ISBN-13: 978-1-949001-56-3 ebook edition

Waterside Productions

Waterside Productions
2055 Oxford Ave.
Cardiff, CA 92007

Table of Contents

LET'S BEGIN

Showing our children how to recognize and regulate their emotions is a crucial piece of successful parenting and teaching. As young educators, we never imagined the time required to develop social-emotional skills in their students. These abilities are "recognized, valued, and supported by ever-expanding research as an important contributor to behavioral improvements, academic achievement, and overall factors of long-term success,"[1] but how can educators and parents find the time in their overloaded schedules to teach self-awareness, empathy, and optimism? The purpose of *Brain Awakes* is to provide a practical way to equip all children with these life skills.

With this straightforward guide, you will be able to lead your children using breath, balance, and reflection. The path of the book follows a developmentally appropriate progression, which starts with children's inner-environment and leads to their relationship with the world around them.

As they practice the art of metacognition, watch their relationships with themselves and others flourish.

Every activity in *Brain Awakes* will occupy less than five minutes and provide a much needed mental break. The reflection section will serve as a guide for valuable conversations with your children. Taking the time to collaborate and reflect will generate greater social-emotional growth.

Our shared devotion to this journey will yield a needed sense of awareness, while inspiring a more compassionate and connected community-one activity at a time.

FOUNDATIONS

If this is your first time practicing mindfulness activities, you are in the right place. Each activity is designed to engage you and your children in interactive learning.

"Tell me and I forget,
teach me and I remember,
involve me and I learn."
—Benjamin Franklin

Let's Balance

Let's Balance activities will get your children up and moving. These pages involve spatial awareness to uncover their connection with their mind, heart, and body.

Let's Breathe

Let's Breathe activities will bring you and your children back to the present moment. On these pages, children will be guided through a mental exploration of their inner and outer environments. These activities will develop an awareness of how they think, feel, and act.

"Mindfulness and yoga are good ways of helping young people develop self-control and calm down," [Hank] Resnik says. "Kids are cognitively able to control themselves."[2]

Let's Balance
- energize -

Crocodile Pose

Lie down on your belly. Cross your arms and place your hands underneath your shoulders. Rest your head on your arms. Think of a crocodile stretching out and relaxing in the sun.

Pull your legs together like a crocodile tale.
Press your hands into the floor, and lift your chest.

Breathe in, look right.
Breathe out, look left.

Breathe in and come back to center.
Return to starting position and repeat.

Let's Reflect:

1. Turn and ask a neighbor when a crocodile might need to stretch its body?
2. How did you feel before and after moving your body with your breathing?
3. What part of your body did you feel stretching?

Brain Awakes

Let's Breathe
- relax -

Notice You're Breathing

Sit up tall. You can sit cross-legged or with your legs straight out in front of you. Your hands can rest on your legs. When you're comfortable, close your eyes.

Let's notice when our breathing starts and stops.
Take a deep breath in through your nose, then breathe out through your mouth.

Do this 2 times thinking "in" as you inhale through your nose and "out" as you exhale through your mouth.

Now, close your lips.
Breathe in and out slowly through your nose for 30 seconds.

Let's Reflect:

1. Open your eyes and turn to tell a friend how you're feeling right now.
2. What was challenging about focusing on your breathing?
3. What are some other things besides breathing that you do all the time without even thinking about it?

Let's Balance
- energize -

Upward Facing Dog

Come into a crocodile pose—lie on your belly with your hands underneath your shoulders.

Breathe in, press your hands into the floor until your arms are straight, and lift your chest.

Breathe out, and come back down to crocodile pose.

Inhale up. Exhale down.

Let's Reflect:

1. Turn to a neighbor and talk about why you think this pose is called upward facing dog.
2. Which part of your body did you feel stretching?
3. When do you think you might need to stretch those muscles again?

Brain Awakes

Let's Breathe
- focus -

Where Is Your Breath?

Sit tall, and close your eyes.

Go ahead and take a nice deep breath in and out through your nose.

Continue these deep, peaceful breaths.

As students breathe, ask these questions:
When you breathe in deeply, where do you feel your breath? Do you feel your breath in your nose or on your lips? Are your shoulders or ribs moving as you breathe deeply? Is your belly filling up and emptying?

Let's Reflect:

1. Open your eyes and turn to tell a friend where you could feel your breath.
2. Do you think you have a deeper breath by filling up your chest with air or your belly?
3. How can a deep breath change the way you are feeling?

Let's Balance
- relax -

Downward Facing Dog

Start in an upward facing dog. Lie on your belly with your hands on the floor and lift your chest.

Press into your hands, and push your hips to the sky. Look between your legs, and let your shoulders relax.

Bend your knees, and stretch your doggy tail up to the sky. Wag your tail from side to side, stretching the sides of your body.

Let's Reflect:

1. Turn and tell a neighbor about a time you saw a dog stretch.
2. How does being upside down help reset the way you feel?
3. Can you think of a time when you would need to reset the way you feel?

Let's Breathe
- relax -

Belly Breathing

Stand up tall with your back straight.

Put your right hand on your belly, and close your eyes.

When you breathe in, fill your belly like a balloon. When you breathe out, deflate your belly.

Take 5 deep and controlled breaths with your hand resting on your belly.

Let's Reflect:

1. Open your eyes and turn to tell a friend how your belly felt as you took your deep breaths.
2. Did you like filling up your belly or deflating your belly more? Why?
3. We also fill ourselves up with emotions. What emotion do you want to be full of? Why?

EMOTIONAL AWARENESS

Emotional awareness is the cornerstone of healthy relationships. The practices in this book "have been linked with improvements in self-regulation in adults, children, and adolescents."[3]

Inner Environment: Recognizing our internal emotions creates a sense of ownership of our hearts. When we teach children how to tune in to their inner environments, we give them the ability to understand how they feel. This understanding leads them to the responsibility of regulating themselves and ultimately controlling how they respond to their surroundings.

Outer Environment: Once our children become aware of the world *within* them, they can then begin to consider the feelings of others. The art of empathy is a skill that must be modeled and taught. It has the ability to transform the way our children think and act.

Tips:

- When reflecting with your children, encourage honesty by creating a safe space for them to express their thoughts and feelings.
- Model a healthy internal dialogue to guide their inner-transformation.
- Prompt emotional awareness discussions about events that happen throughout the day.

Self-Awareness

As you help students understand the emotions in themselves, give them encouragement to acknowledge their feelings. Gently challenge them to be curious about their inner environment as they practice confronting their emotions with a deeper sense of independence and responsibility.

Self-awareness is the ability to notice how we feel within ourselves and the community in which we live. Our emotions play a key role in how we learn and collaborate.

Taking responsibility for our feelings provides us with a way to handle the emotions that travel through us. While a major problem might require action, a less severe issue can simply be felt and let go.

Tips:

- As you begin a new exercise, remind your students to come in with an open mind.
- Create excitement about the activity by being curious about what you might learn.
- Remind your children that we are not our emotions; rather, our emotions are simply feelings that move through us.

Let's Balance
- focus -

What's Alive in You?

Find a seat on the floor.

Have you ever noticed that
feelings can grow? We get to choose what feelings grow
inside of us.

Balance on your bottom, and lift your feet. Spread your
fingers wide like flower petals, and wave hello with your
hands. If you lose your balance, hold onto your legs.

Breathe in and open your flower petals. Imagine growing a
feeling flower. You can grow a happy flower, an excited
flower, a still flower, or any other feeling you want to bring
with you throughout the day.

Let's Reflect:

1. Turn to your neighbor and share what feeling was alive in the flower
you grew.
2. If that feeling flower was real, what color would it be? Why?
3. What can you do to keep this feeling flower alive and healthy?

Brain Awakes

Let's Breathe

- focus -

Pace of Breath

Sit up tall, and close your eyes.

Just breathe for one minute. Pay attention to how you are breathing, but don't change it.

Can you hear your breath?
Is it fast and short?
Is it slow and deep?
Don't change your breath. Just notice it.

Feel your breathing. What makes it fast or slow?

Let's Reflect:

1. Open your eyes and turn to a friend. Describe to him or her how you were breathing.
2. When might you breathe quickly? When would you breathe slowly?
3. How would your breathing be alike or different if you felt relaxed instead of angry?

Let's Balance
- relax -

Watering Your Garden

Stand up straight with your
hands over your heart.

Take two deep breaths.

Then, pretend to hold a
watering can. Breathe deeply
as you slowly raise your hands
all the way above your head.

Slowly tilt your thumbs down toward your head, and pour
the water over you. Imagine how refreshing the cool water
feels.

Now, guide your hands down back to your heart. Take one
deep breath.

Let's Reflect:

1. Turn to a neighbor, and share about a time that you got water
splashed on you.
2. How did it feel to stretch and reach as high as you can?
3. If you could grow any emotion you wanted, which one would you
grow tall and strong? Why?

Let's Breathe
- relax -

Feeling your Favorite Color

Sit tall, and close your eyes.

Think of a color you really like.

Breathe in deeply, and imagine your body is filling up with your favorite color.

Take slow deep breaths.

Watch your body fill up from the top of your head all the way to your toes.

Let's Reflect:

1. Open your eyes and turn to tell a friend what color you chose to fill up with.
2. What emotion did you feel as you imagined yourself filling up with that color?
3. If you were angry, what color would you fill up with?

Let's Balance

- energize -

Charge like a Lizard

Did you know that
lizards charge their
energy by sitting in
the sun?

Step into a big lunge with one foot back and one foot
forward. Bend your front knee. Then, reach your hands to
lay next to your front foot.

Breathe in the energy from the sun, and breathe out as you
relax your muscles.

Jump (or step), and switch your feet.
Breathe and charge.

Let's Reflect:

1. Turn to your neighbors, and ask them their favorite part about this
pose.
2. What was difficult about this activity?
3. What part of the day do you feel sleepy? Could you charge like a
lizard to help energize yourself?

Let's Breathe

- focus -

Feeling the Breath

Sit tall, and put your hand just below your nose.

Now, close your eyes, and breathe in and out slowly through your nose. Notice how the breath feels on your hand.

Take five deep breaths like this.

Where can you feel it?
Is it soft or strong?
Feel the temperature of your breath.
Is it cool or warm?

Let's Reflect:

1. Open your eyes and turn to tell a friend about the way your breath felt on your hand.
2. How do you think your breathing would feel if you were angry? Happy? Sad? Excited?
3. How do you think a friend would be feeling if you saw him or her breathing very quickly?

Let's Balance
- focus -

Hero's Pose

Find a place to sit on your knees. Rest your hands on your legs and sit up tall.

Picture a hero and think of why you admire him or her. Is this person brave, kind, or helpful?

Close your eyes, and breathe.

Let your back grow tall with each breath you take. Feel your body growing strong.

Do you feel your inner hero?

Let's Reflect:

1. Tell a neighbor what hero you chose and why.
2. What traits do you feel in your body as you sit up tall?
3. How can you be a hero for someone younger or older than you?

Let's Breathe
- energize -

Color the Walls

Look at the walls around us. Sit tall, take a deep breath, and close your eyes.

Let's pretend to change the color of our room. We are going to take five deep breaths. Each time we take a breath, we will change the color.

Breathe in, and imagine the walls are turning blue. Breathe out, and erase the color.

Repeat with orange, green, red, and yellow.

Let's Reflect:

1. Open your eyes and turn to tell a friend which color made you feel the happiest? Why?
2. Did you and your friend choose the same color?
3. Did any colors make you feel differently?

Self-Regulation

Throughout our day, we experience a variety of emotions. Self-regulation is the learned ability to control the way we respond to emotions that arise naturally.

Self-regulation can be difficult for children to master without the awareness of their breathing. However, by educating children about the inherent tools within themselves, they can independently gauge their mental states.

Understanding our breathing enables us to act with intention rather than react with emotion. A slow, regular breath exhibits a calm and focused state, while a fast, irregular breath is a signal of a stress response. Once children become aware of this difference, they can proactively answer to their emotions.

Tips:

- Tell children their breathing is their superpower that lets them know how they are feeling.
- Set expectations for children to stay in control of their minds and bodies during the energizing activities. You may even want to use a timer.
- Give your children time to soak in the activity when it is finished. All emotions are welcome and should be respected by all.

Let's Balance
- energize -

Volcano Pose

Squat down low, and squeeze your
knees with your arms.

Explode and jump into the air,
while reaching your arms out wide
in—3, 2, 1!

Get down low, and squeeze your
knees again.
Explode on 3, 2, 1! Repeat this a few times.

Now, breathe in and out slowly to relax your body. Deep
breaths are a way to regulate ourselves when we are tense.

Let's Reflect:

1. Tell a neighbor what you would do if you saw a volcano explode.
2. Why do you think this activity is called volcano pose?
3. When your body feels like a volcano, what can you do to cool
yourself down? Could you use your breathing?

Brain Awakes

Let's Breathe
- relax -

Calm and Relaxed

Today, we will be saying some words silently in our heads.

Sit tall, and close your eyes.

As we breathe in, we will say to ourselves, "I am calm," and as we breathe out, we will say, "I am relaxed."

Breathe in, "I am calm."
Breathe out, "I am relaxed."

Breathe deeply and repeat this five times.

Let's Reflect:

1. Open your eyes and turn to tell a friend about a time you were really relaxed.
2. What is the difference between feeling stressed and feeling relaxed?
3. If you were stressed, could you remind yourself of these words to help you feel more calm?

Let's Balance
- focus -

Cool Down the Lava

Remember our volcano pose? Stand up tall, and close your eyes. Let's pretend we are a volcano that already exploded.

Be still. Reach your arms up, and wiggle your fingers. Tap your fingers lightly on your head like rain that is falling on your volcano.

Let the rain flow through your arms, down your legs, and all the way to your feet.

Now, bring your hands to your shoulders and give yourself a hug. Let the water flow freely to your heart.

Let's Reflect:

1. Turn to tell a neighbor how you felt during this activity.
2. When might you need to do this activity again?
3. Think of one person you want to teach this activity to and explain why.

Brain Awakes

Let's Breathe
- focus -

Five Fingers, Five Breaths

Sit tall, and look at your hand. Comfortably spread out your fingers like when you show the number five.

Starting on the outside of your thumb, breathe in, and trace up your thumb. Breathe out, and slide down your thumb.

Breathe in, and trace up your pointer finger. Breathe out, and slide down your pointer finger.

Continue tracing the rest of your fingers to the pace of your breath.

Let's Reflect:

1. We followed the up and down rhythm of our breathing. Turn to tell a friend if your rhythm was slow and calm or fast and tense.
2. What was challenging about using your hand to follow your breathing?
3. How could you use this activity to help you calm down when you are upset?

Let's Balance

- focus -

Boat Pose

Let's go on a voyage!

Start by sitting down.
Lift your feet, and balance
on your bottom.

Now, pretend to row your
boat.

Row slowly.
Now, row quickly!

Okay, let's row to the pace of our breathing.

Let's Reflect:

1. Turn to your neighbor and share what happened to your body when
you rowed your boat quickly?
2. What happened when you slowed down?
3. Why is it important to slow down occasionally during the day?

Let's Breathe
- relax -

Lie Down and Breathe

For today, you will need an object that is smaller than a book.

Find space to lie flat on your back, and put the object on your belly.

We are going to take big belly breaths today. As we breathe in, try to make your object reach the ceiling. As we breathe out, let your belly fall back to its resting spot.

Close your eyes, and take five controlled big-belly breaths. Follow the pace of your breathing.
"In," "Out;" "In," "Out;" "In," "Out;" ...

Let's Reflect:

1. Open your eyes and turn to tell a friend how you kept your object balanced.
2. Do you think big belly breaths can help you regulate your emotions? Why or why not?
3. When might you be able to use this activity to help you feel calm and in control?

Let's Balance
- relax -

Cooling Down the Mind

Spread out so your arms
can't reach a neighbor.
Then, step your feet wide
apart.

Put your hands on your
head, and thank your brain
for working so hard. Now,
let's create a fan to cool
down our minds.

Reach out wide with your hands, and carefully rotate your
arms in a circle to cool down your mind.

Keep breathing and fanning. Let your arms slow down as
your brain slows down.

Let's Reflect:

1. Turn to tell a neighbor how your brain feels after cooling it off.
2. Even though your arms were moving, were you able to give your
brain a break?
3. Describe a safe time to use this throughout the day.

Brain Awakes

Let's Breathe
- relax -

Peace is Here

Today, we will be saying some words silently in our heads.

Sit tall, and close your eyes.

Breathing in, we will say, "I am here."
Breathing out, we will say, "I am peace."
Breathe in, "I am here."
Breathe out, "I am peace."

Breathe deeply, and repeat these words five times.

Let's Reflect:

1. Open your eyes and turn to tell a friend what peace feels like to you.
2. What is the opposite of peace?
3. What could you say to yourself to help you find peace in a difficult situation?

Empathy

Empathy is the single most important skill that can be learned. When children feel heard, seen, and valued; they radiate the confidence and compassion that elevates those around them. We not only have the ability to create an environment for children to believe in themselves but also to give them the capacity to do the same for others.

By explicitly teaching our children about body language, facial expressions, and tone of voice; we can foster the connection they have with themselves and the world around them.

These activities are designed to inspire collaboration and listening. The time you invest in this section will pay dividends as your children develop their ability to empathize.

Tips:

- During your day, ask children how they think someone (a friend or a book character) is feeling and why.
- Encourage your children to take responsibility for their emotions and respect the emotions of others.
- Model empathy by saying, "I see that you're feeling ___ because _____. That must be ___."

Let's Balance
- energize -

Table Pose

Stand up tall.

Breathe in, and reach
your hands to the sky.
Now breathe out, and
bend forward resting
your hands right above
your knees.

Make your back as flat as you can, and pretend like your
teacher is going to balance a glass of water on you like a
table.
As you press your hands on your legs, can you feel your
back stretch long?

Do this pose with a friend: stand shoulder to shoulder.
Resting your hands on the tops of your knees, make a table
together. Remember to keep your backs flat so the glass
doesn't spill!

Let's Reflect:

1. Tell your neighbor how you could make your table stronger or
weaker.
2. What do you think it means to have someone's back?
3. What can you do to have a friend's back?

Let's Breathe

- focus -

Friends Have Feelings

Sit tall, and close your eyes. Imagine your best friends.

How would they look if they were feeling sad?
How would they sound if they were mad?

How do you know if they are nervous?
What do they look like when they are happy?

Do you look the same way when you have those emotions?

Let's Reflect:

1. Open your eyes and turn to a friend. How do you know the way someone else is feeling?
2. How do you feel when your friend is upset?
3. What are some ways you could help a friend who is feeling nervous?

Let's Balance

- focus -

Grass in the Wind

Stand up. Feel your feet on the floor, and imagine growing roots deep into the ground.

Reach up high, and place your hands together.

Pretend you are a blade of grass in the wind, swaying side to side. As you feel the wind blowing you side to side, feel your strong roots beneath you.

Pretend like the wind is blowing hard, and keep your roots strong in the ground.

Let's Reflect:

1. Turn and tell a neighbor where you felt your body stretch during this pose.
2. Have you ever been challenged by those around you?
3. How can you stay rooted like grass blowing in the wind, strong and connected?

Brain Awakes

Let's Breathe
- relax -

Cloud Breathing

Sit tall, and close your eyes. Imagine that you are a cloud on a beautiful day.

Breathe in, and imagine yourself floating. Breathe out as you move through the sky.

Feel the warmth of the sun shining on your face. Breathe softly like the clouds.

Keep breathing like this for one minute.

Let's Reflect:

1. Open your eyes and turn to tell a friend what the coolest part about being a cloud would be.
2. Would you rather be a cloud on a sunny day or a rainy day? Why?
3. Just like a cloud, we have rainy and sunny days. What are some of our sunny emotions? What are some of our rainy emotions?

Let's Balance

- energize -

Candle of Hope

Lie down on your back.

Lift your feet up to the sky, and pretend your legs are a candle.

Think about what might make your candle dim throughout the day. Lower your feet to the ground.

Now, think about what keeps you going and shining bright during your day. Raise your legs high into the air.

Let's Reflect:

1. Turn to a neighbor and discuss how we can remember to keep our candle shining brightly throughout the day.
2. What do you do when your candle feels dim?
3. What might be a sign that someone's candle is dim? What can you do to help?

Let's Breathe
- energize -

Smile Breathing

If you lose your focus during today's activity, remember to come back to your breath.

Sit tall, and close your eyes.

We are going to take 5 deep breaths. Every time we breathe in, we are going to smile a little bigger. By the end of the five breaths, we are going to have a giant smile on our faces.

Breathe in, and slowly start to smile.
Breathe out, and feel your heart fill with joy.
Breathe in, and smile.
Breathe out, and be happy.
Do this for five deep breaths.

Let's Reflect:

1. Open your eyes and turn to tell a friend what smiling feels like.
2. What happens when you see someone else smiling?
3. Is there another way you can see that people are happy besides their smile?

Let's Balance
- focus -

Chameleon Pose

Did you know that a chameleon can change its body to be the same color as its environment?

Stand up tall, and pretend to hold onto a branch. I'm going to act out an emotion, and you are going to slowly transform your body to blend in with me. We will hold that emotional pose until I call out the next one.

Call out the following emotions, and then act them out.
Examples: excited, stressed, disgusted, shocked, angry, and happy.

Let's Reflect:

1. Turn to a neighbor, and discuss what makes up the environment of our room.
2. How do your emotions affect the environment around us?
3. What type of environment is the easiest for you to work in?

Let's Breathe
- focus -

Loving Kindness: Foe

Have you ever felt unhappy with someone? We are going to practice what we can do to help ourselves forgive him or her.

Sit tall and close your eyes. Breathe deeply and comfortably. Repeat after me quietly aloud, or silently in your head.

"May I be happy." "May I be healthy." "May I be safe."

Keep your eyes closed, but now think of the person with whom you are upset. Picture that person's face and heart.

Repeat after me. "May you be happy." "May you be healthy." "May you be safe."

Let's Reflect:

1. Turn to tell a friend how it felt to wish those kind things to yourself.
2. How did you feel as you wished those kind things to the person who hurt your heart?
3. Why would we still wish nice things to those who did something unkind?

Empathy

COMMUNITY

"One can acquire everything in solitude,
except character." –Stendhal

All children are a part of an intricate web. They have friends, family members, and role models. As they spend time with their families at home and their friends at school, they are learning how to treat others in their community.

"When students feel positive about their schools and the people in them, they will perform better and have a greater capacity to meet challenges."[2]

In the upcoming sections of *Brain Awakes*, we will explore a compassionate approach to friendships, expand problem solving skills, and examine our differences—knowing they are a valuable contribution to our communities. This knowledge will alter the mindset of "me" to the mindset of "we."

Tips:

- Continue your discussions on empathy as you explore the topic of community.
- Emphasize how special our differences are.
- When issues arise throughout the day, consider having a discussion using the language and skills found in the upcoming activities.

Friendship

Forming bonds naturally is imperative to our children's learning and development. As a parent or teacher, our job is to guide children toward being an honest and true friend by modeling the behavior we want to see. This includes the practice of listening, appreciating our differences, and inquiring about how we can best treat ourselves and others.

Approaching friendship with the "Golden Rule" creates a mirror for kids to become the type of friends they want to be. As you encourage your children to form bonds with others, remind them of their potential to be inclusive *and included*. This contributes to creating a better family, classroom, society, and world.

Tips:

- If a child says he or she has no friends, discuss what a good friend is and how they can embody that person.
- In partnering activities, challenge kids to put their friend first.
- Throughout the day, point out moments when children are being good friends:
  "I see _____ being a good friend by _____."

Let's Balance
- focus -

Plank Pose

Are you ready to discover how strong you are?

Lie down like you are about to do a pushup. Make sure your shoulders are over your wrists and your fingers are spread wide. Keep your arms straight, and push all your fingers into the floor.

Breathe in and breathe out.
Do you feel your body starting to warm up?

Come down to your knees to take a break. Brainstorm with your neighbor how to make this pose easier.
Now, try the plank pose one more time.

Let's Reflect:

1. Turn to a neighboring group, and share what you did to make the plank pose easier.
2. How does brainstorming with others help you solve problems?
3. Why is it important to listen to your friend's ideas when you're talking together?

Let's Breathe
- energize -

Bright Light

Sit tall, and close your eyes.

Imagine that you are a lamp in a dark room. You are shining in the darkness around you.

Breathe deeply, and let the light fill you up.

Now, imagine another lamp turns on and the room is a little brighter. After that, another lamp and another turn on. Soon the whole room is lit up and bright as can be.

Breathe in, and imagine the room filling with our brightness.

Let's Reflect:
1. Turn to tell a friend how you felt when you were the only lamp in the dark room.
2. How did you feel when other lamps started making the room brighter and brighter?
3. How could you brighten up your room with the choices you make?

Let's Balance
- focus -

Elevator

Pretend to step into an elevator. Put your feet together, and squat down low. We are on floor 1. Get ready to jump up to floor 2.

When I say "Ding," press the button for floor 2, and jump!
   "DING!"

Now you're on floor 2. You are in the middle. Bend your knees like you're sitting in a chair.

Get ready to jump up to floor 3. When I say, "Ding," press the button for floor 3, and jump! "DING!"
After that, ride the elevator all the way to the ground floor.

Let's Reflect:

1. Turn to your neighbor and discuss a time you rode on an elevator.
2. Why is it safest to ride an elevator with a friend instead of by yourself?
3. What else is safer to do with a friend?

Let's Breathe
- focus -

Loving Kindness: Loved One

Think of someone you love—maybe someone in your family. Sit tall, and close your eyes. Breathe deeply and comfortably.

You may say these words quietly aloud, or silently in your head. "May I be happy." "May I be healthy." "May I be safe." "May I be happy." "May I be healthy." "May I be safe."

Keep your eyes closed, but now think of your loved one. Picture that person's face and their warmth.

Repeat after me. "May you be happy." "May you be healthy." "May you be safe." "May you be happy." "May you be healthy." "May you be safe."

Let's Reflect:

1. Open your eyes and turn to tell a friend what it felt like to wish yourself those kind things again.
2. How did you feel when you said those kind words to your loved one?
3. How can you share joy with your friends and family?

Let's Balance

- focus -

Making Soup

Sit across from a partner, and put your feet toe to toe. Then, spread your feet apart. This is your soup bowl.

Talk to your partner about what type of soup you want to make, and start adding the ingredients. When you are finished, link hands, and stir the pot.

Feel the stretch on your legs as you work together to follow a smooth rhythm.

Go slowly so you don't spill the soup!

Let's Reflect:

1. Turn to a neighboring group and ask them what type of soup they made.
2. What could you do if your neighbor started getting tired?
3. If you made a giant bowl of soup, with whom would you share it and why?

Let's Breathe
- focus -

Loving Kindness: Grade Levels

Today, we will be saying some words together. You can say them quietly aloud, or silently in your head.

Sit tall, and close your eyes. Breathe deeply and comfortably. Repeat after me, "May I be happy." "May I be healthy." "May I be safe."

Keep your eyes closed, but now we will think of our kindergarten-aged friends. Picture their faces and their hearts. Repeat after me. "May you be happy." "May you be healthy." "May you be safe."

Repeat for all grade levels in your building, including your own.

Let's Reflect:

1. Open your eyes and turn to tell a friend how you feel when you say those words.
2. Why are we saying these kind words to everyone—even people whom we don't know?
3. How can you continue to build a community that is loving and kind?

Let's Balance

- energize -

Bicycle

Sit down, and face a partner.

Lift your feet in the air, and put them toe to toe with your partner. Keep them spread like you're sitting on a bicycle.

Start to slowly pedal your bicycle feet.

Can you work together to pedal at the same speed as your partner?

Let's Reflect:

1. Discuss with your neighbor the best part about working as a team.
2. What is the hardest part about working with others?
3. What can you do to make sure everyone on your team works together?

Let's Breathe
- relax -

I Am Safe and Loved

Today, we will be saying some words together in our heads as we breathe.

Close your eyes, and sit tall.

As we breathe in deeply, we will think, "I am safe." As we breathe out, we will think, "I am loved."

Breathing in, "I am safe."
Breathing out, "I am loved."

Repeat these kind words for five breaths.

Let's Reflect:

1. Turn to a friend and tell him or her what makes you feel safe and why.
2. Who is someone who makes you feel loved?
3. How can you make a friend feel safe or loved?

Problem Solving

If your children spill a glass of juice, cleaning it up for them will not teach them how to solve that problem in the future. Whether it's a math problem, a disagreement with a friend, or a spilled glass of juice, it is our jobs as parents and teachers to guide our children and help them become problem solvers.

Kids who learn how to problem solve tend to use these skills toward not only physical challenges but mental and emotional challenges as well.

In the upcoming activities, invite your children to channel their inner hero. Problem solving takes both curiosity and courage. Whether it be falling during plank pose or falling into an emotion, remind them that their efforts will continue to teach them as they try again.

Tips:

- Praise your children for having the courage to face a problem.
- When tackling a large problem, admire and encourage the effort in the steps it takes while letting go of the end result.
- Remember that not all children have witnessed healthy problem-solving skills. This is a slow but worthwhile journey.

Let's Balance

- energize -

Airplane Pose

Today, we get to pose like an airplane. Are you ready to take off? Let's go!

Start by balancing on one foot.
Lift your floating foot back and stretch your arms out like an airplane.

To help you balance, try to keep your eyes on something still. Then, slow down your breathing.

Let's Reflect:

1. Turn to your neighbor and share which foot was easier to balance on.
2. What helped you balance on one leg?
3. What is something you could do to help you balance on the more difficult side?

Brain Awakes

Let's Breathe

- energize -

Favorite Holiday

Sit tall, and close your eyes.

Imagine your favorite holiday. Think about what you do. What do you get to eat?

Picture with whom you enjoy spending time, and notice how your heart feels right now.

Holidays can also be stressful. Have you ever had a problem during a holiday? Was your family able to work together?

Let's Reflect:

1. Open your eyes and turn to tell a friend what your favorite holiday is and why?
2. Why is it important that you can work together to solve problems with your family?
3. What are some things you can do to help your family solve a problem?

Let's Balance
- energize -

Frog Pose

Spread your feet out wide, and bend your knees like a frog.

Exhale out all your air, and prepare to inhale.
Inhale as you fly into the sky.

Land on your feet quietly, like a frog on a lily pad.

Keep hopping to the rhythm of your breath.

Let's Reflect:

1. Ask your neighbors what they did to make a quiet leap.
2. How might our quiet or loud landing affect the people around us?
3. Can you think of a time when you were mindful of the people around you?

Let's Breathe
- relax -

The Wind

Sit tall, and close your eyes.

Let's imagine you are a leaf blowing in the wind, tumbling and floating across the grass.

Blow deep breaths like the strong wind!

Now, let the wind and your breathing start to slow down. Your imaginary leaf settles and rests.

Keep your eyes closed, and breathe calmly.

Let's Reflect:

1. Discuss with a friend about a time you have felt like a tumbling leaf.
2. Sometimes we feel still while others are like a tumbling leaf. What can you do if someone is being distracting?
3. If you were getting pushed around (like the leaf in the wind), how could you solve the problem with kindness?

Let's Balance
- focus -

Tree Pose

Lift up each of your toes, and put them down one at a time. Feel your whole foot connected to the floor.

Now, find a still place to look, and start to lift one leg. Put your lifted foot above or below your knee on your standing leg. Use your hands to help you stay balanced.

Keep your chest lifted, and when you are balanced, lift your arms to grow your branches.

Let's Reflect:

1. Turn to a neighbor and share how you stayed balanced on one foot.
2. What did you do if you started to lose your balance?
3. If you start to have a problem with a friend, what should you do before you fall and the problem becomes worse?

Let's Breathe
- focus -

A Time of Helping

Sit tall, and close your eyes.

Think about a time that you helped someone. Imagine you are back in that moment helping that person.

What did you do? How did you help him or her?

What did it feel like to help another person? Did you notice how you made him or her feel?

Let's Reflect:

1. Open your eyes and turn to tell a friend how you helped someone.
2. Why do you think we feel good when we help others? How do we feel when we hurt others?
3. If you make a mistake when solving a problem, who could you ask for help?

Let's Balance
- focus -

Eagle Pose

Stand up tall, and keep
your chest high.

Have you ever noticed
how an eagle flies high
above and can see things
differently from us?

Focus on a point on the wall that is not moving to keep you
balanced. Bend your knees slightly, and wrap one leg
around the other. Then, bring your hands to your hips like
wings.

Breathe in, and feel the strength of the eagle. Breathe out,
and notice everything around you as you soar.

Let's Reflect:

1. Turn to your neighbor and talk about the most difficult part of this
pose.
2. If you have a problem with a friend, how could you use a different
point of view to solve the issue?
3. How can it be helpful to use a different point of view if you're stuck
in a challenge?

Brain Awakes

Let's Breathe
- relax -

I Believe and Trust

Close your eyes, and sit tall.

Today, we are going to be thinking some words together as we breathe.

As we inhale, we will think, "I believe in myself."
As we exhale, we will think, "I trust myself."

Repeat these phrases with five deep breaths.

"I believe in myself. I trust myself."

Let's Reflect:

1. Open your eyes and turn to tell a friend what it means to trust yourself.
2. Have you ever done something you shouldn't have and felt your heart or tummy turning and feeling weird afterward?
3. It is important that we trust ourselves. What does it feel like when we want to say yes to something? What does it feel like when we should say no to something?

Accepting Differences

Learning how to celebrate our unique differences creates a more comfortable and productive home, classroom, and community.

As our children grow, they begin to observe and question the world around them. We have daily opportunities to model acceptance and openness towards our differences.

This can be challenging for adults and children alike. Once we allow ourselves and others to make different choices, think different thoughts, and have different beliefs; we can develop a greater sense of self, rooted in experience.

During these activities, we will reflect on how our unique differences contribute to making us stronger as a whole.

Tips:

- When you hear children giving different opinions, point out the value in both perspectives.
- Don't forget that while we celebrate our differences, we can also enjoy what we have in common.
- Children should feel confident in themselves and compassionate for others during these activities.

Let's Balance
- energize -

Shining the Heart

Slouch forward, and be lazy. Now, stand up super tall! Lift your chest. Pull your shoulders back.

Now, find the middle. Stand up tall with the top of your head lifting to the sky. As you close your eyes, imagine the sun is shining in your heart.

With every breath you take, the sun gets a little brighter.

Breathe in, and fill up with light. Breathe out, and let the sunshine fill from your chest to your arms. Feel it glowing and radiating.

Let's Reflect:

1. Turn to a neighbor, and explain what you imagined when you closed your eyes. What did you feel in your heart?
2. Do we all feel a little bit different during this exercise?
3. How can you remind your partner that their heart is special?

Let's Breathe
- focus -

Soaring and Breathing

Sit tall, close your eyes, and breathe deeply.

Think of the most beautiful bird you've ever seen flying in the sky. Imagine that you are that bird.

Breathe and soar. Feel the wind on your wings. You're as light as the air.

Look down. What do you see from up in the sky? Notice as much as you can as you fly.

Let's Reflect:

1. Open your eyes and turn to tell a friend what the hardest part about being a bird would be.
2. Some birds fly, and others run or swim. What is special about birds that swim? What about birds that run? What is special about birds that fly?
3. What is something special that you can do?

Let's Balance

- energize -

Camel Pose

Have you ever noticed how camels have different sized humps on their backs? This is where they store water!

Stand on your knees. Reach your hands back to your heels, and lift your head up and back.

Take a few deep breaths and fill up the front side of your body with air.

Breathe deeply throughout your entire body, and see if you can feel the stretch in your shoulders.

Let's Reflect:

1. Turn to your neighbor and talk about how the camel pose felt. Did you feel the same or different?
2. What can you do when you need something different from those around you?
3. What happens when you communicate what you need?

Brain Awakes

Let's Breathe
- relax -

Tree Breathing

Sit tall, and close your eyes.

Imagine you are a tree. Your strong roots run deep into the earth. Your limbs grow tall and wide.

Breathe in and out, and feel your strength.

Keep breathing deeply, and imagine you are a tree on a beautiful day. Feel the wind on your leaves.

Be still while the kids play below you and the birds fly high above you.

Let's Reflect:

1. Open your eyes and turn to tell a friend what it feels like to be a tree.
2. Are some trees better than others? Why or why not?
3. What do trees do that is important? What do you do that is important?

Let's Balance
- relax -

Rock Pose

Sit down, and grab your knees with your hands.

Pretend you are a rock in an open field. Close your eyes. Breathe deeply and say the words that you need to hear today.

Breathe in your words and breathe out as you hug your knees and lift your head.

I am going to
remind myself:
"I am safe."
"I am loved."
"I am well."
"I am awesome."

Let's Reflect:

1. Turn and tell your neighbor how it felt to be still like a rock.
2. What did you need to remind yourself today?
3. What is something awesome about your neighbor?

Let's Breathe
- focus -

Personal Paradise

Sit tall, close your eyes, and breathe deeply.

Think of your most favorite place. It could be a room, a chair, or a place you visit. Think about it. Imagine you are there.

What do you notice? Can you see what is on the walls or on the ground? What do you smell? What types of noises do you hear?

Breathe in and out, and notice how it feels to be there.

Let's Reflect:

1. Open your eyes and turn to tell a neighbor why that place is your favorite.
2. Did your friend have a different favorite place? Is it okay if you and your friend like different things?
3. What else is different about you and your partner?

Let's Balance

- energize -

Bridge Pose

Find a seat on the floor, and put your hands on the ground behind you.

Press your feet down, and lift your hips.

Breathe in, and reach your hips high.
Breathe out, and feel your bridge stable and strong.

Let's Reflect:

1. Turn to your neighbor and share how you could be strong and stable for others.
2. What's important to remember when you're helping others solve problems?
3. Share one strength you add to your team.

Let's Breathe
- relax -

Pebble in the River

Sit tall, close your eyes, and breathe deeply.

Imagine you are a pebble resting at the bottom of a river. Sit and relax as the water flows. Notice all of the different fish swimming by happily.

Look up toward the surface. Watch for small fish and big fish, frogs, little bugs, turtles, and maybe even a beaver.

As your pebble rests happily on the river, feel the cool water rushing by.

Let's Reflect:

1. Open your eyes and turn to tell a friend what animals you imagined in the river.
2. How are all the different animals in the river kind of like all the different types of people in our world?
3. What is nice about having friends who are all a little different from you?

GOAL SETTING

By now, your children have begun to understand that they are a special part of our community. Moving forward, the question becomes how are they going to impact the world in which they live?

Our world is full of obstacles and distractions. When we are told we can't achieve something, having a growth mindset reminds us we can.

"Research indicates that skills like communication, problem solving, teamwork, and self-esteem are not only important for success, but are also important for enabling young people to become better learners in general."[4]

By teaching our children how to set and accomplish goals, they develop the power to keep their chin high even when they feel like giving up. Nothing can stop children who believe in themselves.

Tips:

- Let your children create a goal that they want to accomplish, and then break their goal into smaller steps.
- Model positive self-talk to keep your children encouraged and motivated.
- Part of goal setting is occasionally failing. Be sure to point out that it's good to take risks and make mistakes.

Optimism & Motivation

Optimism and motivation go hand-in-hand when it comes to human potential. Fostering a sense of confidence creates momentum for children as they prove to themselves that they can achieve anything they put their minds to.

All tasks, big and small, can be tackled with a positive approach. When we are motivated, we know that the outcome will be worth the hard work.

In the upcoming activities, we invite you to create a space of positivity and determination to explore your inner hero. Watch their chests rise with pride as they beam with encouragement.

Let us embody a sense of strength that comes from within. As we trust in our inner hero, we inspire others to do the same.

Tips:

- Knowing you're not alone is motivation in itself. Continue to build a sense of community with your children.
- Collaborate on some options of what you might say to yourself when you're not feeling motivated and optimistic.
- Praise a child when you see him or her being optimistic and motivated.

Let's Balance

- energize -

Superhero Pose

Lie down on your
belly, and stretch
your arms above
your head.

Think of your
favorite superhero.

As you breathe in, lift your arms and legs off the ground.
Fly to the right, to the left, and back to center.

Do this a few times to exercise your superhero.

Let's Reflect:

1. Tell a neighbor your favorite superhero and why.
2. Who has been like a superhero in your life?
3. How can you be a superhero in the classroom? In the school? In our community?

Let's Breathe
- energize -

Just Like a Dandelion

Sit tall, and close your eyes.

Imagine that you have a baby dandelion in front of you that is barely showing above the dirt.

Breathe slowly in through your nose, and imagine the dandelion growing a bit taller. Breathe out through your mouth, and blow all of the seedlings into the wind.

Take four more deep breaths.

As you breathe in and out, watch all of the seedlings float around and land in the grass.

Let's Reflect:

1. Open your eyes and tell a friend how it felt to grow the young dandelion and to spread all of its fuzzies.
2. Just like the dandelion, you're growing, too. What do you want to grow up to be someday?
3. How will working hard help you reach your goals?

Let's Balance
- energize -

Rocket Ship Launch

Squat down as low as you can. Pretend you are a rocket ship. Get ready for launch! Clasp your hands above your head.

Countdown 5...4...3...2...1...Blast off!
Jump and land standing straight up like a rocket ship.

Close your eyes, and take deep breaths like you are flying through space. Imagine passing your busy thoughts like they are clouds.

Watch the clouds fade as you enter outer space.

Let's Reflect:

1. Tell your neighbor how your deep breaths helped you create space in your mind.
2. What gives you energy when you are tired and want to give up?
3. How can you shoot for the stars like a rocket ship?

Brain Awakes

Let's Breathe
- energize -

New Things in Old Spaces

Sit tall, and keep your eyes open.

Today, without talking or pointing, look around and notice five things that you have never really paid attention to before.

You can keep track by counting on your fingers. Once you have found five new things, take five deep breaths. As you breathe, use your pointer finger to trace each of the fingers on your other hand.

Sometimes, new things are right in front of us and we don't even know it. Always keep your eyes open for chances to discover and learn new things.

Let's Reflect:

1. Turn to tell a friend two new things that you noticed today.
2. Even after being in this room so much, how were you able to find new things?
3. Just like these things in the room that have always been here, what is something new you can notice about yourself?

Let's Balance
- relax -

Moon Pose

Lie down on your back.

Reach your arms up, and
stretch to the right.
Put your feet toward the
right side to pretend like
you are a moon.

Take 5 deep breaths.
When your belly rises up,
imagine a glowing light fills
up your body. As you breathe out, let the light dim.

Switch sides after 5 breaths.

Let's Reflect:

1. Turn to your neighbor and discuss how you can share your glowing
light with others today.
2. What is special about the nighttime?
3. What is one thing you are looking forward to today that keeps your
light shining?

Let's Breathe
- energize -

Sun Breathing

Sit tall, close your eyes, and begin to deepen your breathing.

Imagine that you are the sun. You are the warmth of the universe. Your energy is always there, even when it is nighttime!

Breathe in and out, and shine bright.

You are the giant star that is the source of light for our world.

Be bright. Be warm. Be the sun.

Let's Reflect:

1. Open your eyes and turn to tell a friend how you are like the sun.
2. We need the sun's energy and warmth. How can you warm a friend's heart?
3. What is something you can do to shine bright in our classroom?

Let's Balance
- energize -

Waterfall

Have you ever seen a waterfall? Let's pretend to climb up to the top of one.

Start in a low squat position by bending your knees. Let's climb up the rocks!

Climb up and down, finding the wrong path a few times, and keep encouraging your children. If you believe you can, you can! We can do it!

Reach your hands up high and stand on your tippy toes. Make a "shhh" noise as you run your waterfall hands down to the earth.

Let's Reflect:

1. Turn to your neighbor and share a time you've had to make new paths toward your goal.
2. Talk about a time when you overcame a big challenge, and explain what you did to believe in yourself.
3. Share a time when someone cheered you on towards your goal.

Let's Breathe
- energize -

I See Me

Sit tall, close your eyes, and breathe deeply.

Think about your favorite thing to do. It could be at school or at home. Imagine yourself doing it.

How do you feel when you do it?
Do you smile when you're doing your favorite thing?
Do you get to do it with others or by yourself?

Now, imagine yourself all grown up and doing what you love. You're happy and healthy.

Let's Reflect:

1. Open your eyes and turn to tell a friend what your favorite thing to do is.
2. What do you need to be happy and healthy today?
3. Describe a time when you chose to have fun doing something that you didn't really want to do.

Focusing In

Kids have enough energy to move mountains!
Some of the time, they are moving a different mountain than the one we want them to be moving.

When guiding your children towards focusing in, meet them where they are. Look into where their current focus is, and help them shift their concentration.

Just as riding a bike takes practice, so does focus. The upcoming activities are designed to enhance our children's inner ability to focus. It will take time and effort, but this awareness helps children reach their goals.

Tips:

- Be realistic with your children's attention span: it is typically the same number of minutes as their age.
- Remind your children to use their breathing and to focus their eyes as a constant tool to keep them centered and aware.
- An effective way to inspire focus is to present the activity as a game or challenge, discovering what is possible.

Let's Balance

- focus -

Racecar Pose

Racecar drivers go so fast. In order to stay focused on the road, they have to keep their bodies really still and take deep breaths.

Sit down, and put your feet straight out in front of you. Pretend you are holding the steering wheel.

When I say go, press your right foot forward like you are stepping on the gas. Every time we turn, we will take a slow deep breath around the corner of the racetrack!

"Breathe in and focus."
"Breathe out and turn."
Be careful, and stay on the road.

Let's Reflect:

1. Turn to your neighbors, and tell them when you need a deep breath during your day.
2. What transition is the hardest throughout your day?
3. How can you change the way you take the transition to make a smooth turn?

Let's Breathe
- focus -

Hold and Squeeze

For today, find something you can fit in your hand.
Once you have that object, sit tall and close your eyes with it in your hand.

Breathe deeply and slowly.

Feel the weight of your object in your hand. Lightly squeeze it, and feel its shape. Notice it's features and textures.

Now, open your hand flat, and let it just rest in your palm. Take two deep breaths, and just sit with your item.

Let's Reflect:

1. Open your eyes and turn to tell a friend what you noticed about the item you were holding.
2. What happens when you focus on one thing, like the object in your hand?
3. How might focusing on one thing in front of you be helpful? What happens when you try to focus on too many things at once?

Let's Balance
- energize -

Rainbow Pose

Kneel on the floor.
Place your right hand down on the ground, and stick out your opposite foot.

Stretch your floating arm up and over your ear like you are painting a rainbow in the sky.

Do the other side, and breathe in and out with your arm motion as you paint a rainbow in the sky.

Let's Reflect:

1. Turn to your neighbor and talk about what conditions are needed to make a rainbow.
2. If rain and sunlight help make a rainbow, what conditions make a good day?
3. What conditions help you focus?

Brain Awakes

Let's Breathe
- energize -

Silent Search

Sit tall, and keep your eyes open.

When I say a color, try to find something in the room that is that color.

Keep it to yourself, and when you find something, look at it. Then take a deep breath while focusing on what you found.

Slowly call out the following colors:
blue, red, purple, yellow, pink, green

Let's Reflect:

1. Turn to tell a friend one of the items you found, and then discuss what color it was.
2. What did you do to help yourself stay focused during this activity?
3. If you get distracted, how could you refocus yourself without interrupting a friend?

Let's Balance
- focus -

Surfer's Pose

Did you know some surfers go out to the water to clear their mind?

Close your eyes, and notice how your body feels. Remember this feeling. We will talk about it at the end.

Come down to a low push-up position.
Paddle your arms like you are in the water.

When I say, "Wave," press yourself onto your feet as you jump onto your imaginary surfboard. "Ready, WAVE!" Balance on your front foot, balance on your back foot, close your eyes and ride the wave using your arms for balance.

Let's Reflect:

1. Turn to your neighbor and share how you feel after surfing.
2. How did focusing on surfing changed your mood?
3. What foot is easier to balance on? How could you get better at balancing on the other foot?

Brain Awakes

Let's Breathe
- relax -

Hot Air Balloon Breaths

Sit tall, and close your eyes.

Imagine that you are a beautiful hot air balloon high in the sky. You are floating peacefully.

As you breathe in, watch yourself rise higher into the blue sky. As you breathe out, gently lower down into the clouds.

Breathe in, and go higher.
Breathe out, and go lower.

Do this a few times until you feel peace inside.

Let's Reflect:

1. Open your eyes and turn to tell a friend what it felt like to be a hot air balloon.
2. Can you think of a reason it would be important to focus while flying a hot air balloon?
3. What could you say to yourself, or what could you do, to keep yourself focused?

Let's Balance
- focus -

Helicopter Pose

Spread out so your arms can't reach a neighbor.

Imagine that you're a helicopter on a windy day. You need to take off safely. Find some extra focus to stay centered as you take off.

Get ready for lift-off!

Take off by slowly twisting in a circle.
Try staying centered by keeping your helicopter lifted up to the sky.

Let's Reflect:

1. Turn to your neighbor and share what types of weather patterns can affect the way a helicopter flies?
2. What conditions in the classroom can make it challenging to do your work?
3. How can you prepare and focus so that your helicopter makes it to your destination?

Let's Breathe
- focus -

Shirt, Arms, and Hands

Sit tall, and close your eyes.

Notice the way your shirt is lying on you. Where is it touching you, and how does it feel?

Take a few deep breaths to focus your attention on yourself.

Notice where your arms are placed. Feel the way they rest.

Try to focus your mental attention on how your hands are resting. Don't move them. Just notice the way they are.

Let's Reflect:

1. Open your eyes and turn to tell a friend where your arms were resting.
2. Which one was the hardest to notice and focus on—your shirt, arms, or hands? Why?
3. How were you able to focus your attention without getting distracted?

Perseverance

Reaching our goals can be challenging, even when we are focused. Obstacles and hurdles can appear frequently. When setbacks begin to feel like total failure, it is much easier to throw in the towel than to stay dedicated to the goal.

Changing our statements from "I can't" to "I can't yet" opens up the opportunity to believe in ourselves. Teaching the value of persistence makes a difficult or time-consuming task seem possible and rewarding.

As we conclude our activities, the last section is meant to be a boost for you and your children. Perseverance is the skill that uncovers the limitless possibilities that lie within ourselves. If you can cultivate this quality in your children, they will be able to conquer any of life's challenges.

Tips:

- Stay encouraging and praise children when you see them persevering through a difficult task.
- If we learn from our failures, they are no longer mistakes.
- Consider looping back around to "Emotional Awareness" when you finish the last activity.

Let's Balance
- focus -

Bird Sipping Water

Stand up, and find a still point to look at for balance. Breathe in deep, and reach up high. Breathe out, and reach your arms behind your back as you sit in an imaginary chair.

Try to balance here in this chair, and use your arms for help. When you are ready, lift up onto your toes like a bird on a perch.

See how many slow breaths you can take while you balance on your toes.

Now do it with a friend, connect hands, stand side-by-side, and balance together!

Let's Reflect:

1. Turn to your neighbor and discuss what was challenging about the bird sipping water pose.
2. This pose was physically challenging. Can you think of something that is mentally challenging?
3. What helped you persevere when you fell?

Let's Breathe
- focus -

Straw Breathing

Sit tall, close your eyes, and take two deep breaths.

Now, grab an imaginary drinking straw. Put the straw to your lips, and act like you are going to take a drink.

Instead, we are going to take straw-breaths. Try to breathe in and out with your straw for thirty seconds.

Set your imaginary straw to the side, and take one deep breath. How do your breaths feel different from normal?

Let's Reflect:

1. Open your eyes and turn to tell a friend what we can say to ourselves to keep on trying even when something is tough.
2. Have you ever pushed through instead of giving up when something got difficult?
3. How can this imaginary straw remind you to persevere?

Let's Balance
- relax -

Cooling Down Lion Pose

When a lion overheats, he opens his mouth to cool down. After he cools down his body, he can begin to run again.

Stand on your knees.
Put your hands up like lion
paws.

Imagine you are a lion that has
just been running for a long time. You are exhausted and need to cool down.

Breathe in through your nose and out through your mouth.

Notice the hot air releasing from your body.

Let's Reflect:

1. Turn to your neighbor and share what other animals open their mouth to cool themselves down.
2. When would the lion pose be helpful? When would the lion pose be inappropriate?
3. When something is challenging, we can get overheated. How can the cooling down lion pose teach you to persevere?

Let's Breathe
- focus -

What Do You Hear?

Sit tall, and close your eyes.

We are going to spend 1 minute in silence. Your job is to breathe deeply and listen to everything you can hear.

Try not to make any noise yourself. Just sit, breathe, and notice everything you can.

I will tell you when the one minute is up.

Let's Reflect:

1. Open your eyes and turn to tell a friend two things that you heard.
2. How might the quiet help you focus? What is uncomfortable about the quiet?
3. It would have been easy to get distracted during this activity. Why is it important that we never give up, even when something is difficult, tiresome, or uncomfortable?

Let's Balance
- relax -

Calm the Storm

Quickly split the children into four groups: Rain, Thunder, Lightning, Air

Teach the rain kids to rub their hands together to make the sound "shhh."
Thunder kids will

stomp their feet. Lightning kids will jump high as they can.
Wind kids will wiggle their arms and blow the air.

Let's all take a deep breath before the storm.
Now, let me hear the rain!
Let's see the wind!
Let's hear the thunder!
Let's see the lightning!
Let's calm the storm with a deep breath.

Let's Reflect:

1. Tell your neighbor what you thought was exciting about that activity.
2. What type of storm or challenge do you face during the day?
3. What can you tell yourself if you need help persevering through a storm?

Brain Awakes

Let's Breathe

- energize -

Blow Up a Balloon

Have you ever had to blow up a balloon? It can be very difficult.

Sit tall, and close your eyes. Pretend you're holding an itty-bitty balloon.

We are going to take big breaths in, and each time we breathe out, our balloon is going to get bigger.

Breathe in, and then breathe out to blow up your balloon a little more.

Take five deep breaths to blow up a big balloon in your hands.

Let's Reflect:

1. Ask a friend if he or she has ever popped a balloon before.
2. Blowing up one balloon isn't difficult, but how would you feel if you had to blow up 100 balloons for a party?
3. If you had to blow up 100 balloons, what would you do to persevere and not give up?

Let's Balance

- energize -

Plant a Big Flower

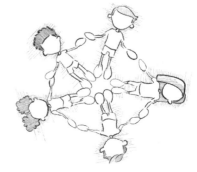

Sit in a circle with everyone's
feet in the middle. Discuss what
is needed for a flower to bloom.

Pretend you are planting seeds
in the middle of the circle with
your hands. First, put your hands on your belly, and
breathe into the sun. Then, put your hands in the sky, and
breathe in the air.

Ask, "Why hasn't the flower bloomed yet?"
Talk about how good things take time and perseverance.

Quietly have everyone lie down and take 5 slow and deep
breaths. As they lie in the circle, point out how each child is
a petal of the big flower!

Let's Reflect:

1. Turn and tell a neighbor about something you've grown.
2. A flower needs certain things to grow. What do you need to grow
healthy?
3. What is one thing that helps you persevere when something takes a
long time?

Let's Breathe
- relax -

Present Moment, Wonderful Moment

Sit tall, and close your eyes.

Today, we will be thinking some words together.

As we breathe in, we will say to ourselves "Present moment." That means right now.
As we breathe out, we will say, "Wonderful moment." That means right now is amazing.

Breath in "Present moment."
Breathe out "Wonderful moment."

Repeat this five times.

Let's Reflect:

1. Open your eyes and turn to tell a friend two things that are wonderful right now.
2. Is it possible to find something wonderful in every moment?
3. When could you say these words to yourself to help you persevere?

MOVING FORWARD

The activities that make up *Brain Awakes* have come to an end; however, our hope is that your life-long journey to empowerment continues. In the upcoming weeks, intentionally weave social-emotional conversations into everyday interactions. Watch for teachable moments, and be prepared to take the time to capture them.

Moving forward, continue to integrate balance and breath. Don't be afraid to repeat activities based on the needs of your children, as they will always generate new findings. Revisiting an activity might even give you a glimpse of their progress. At the very least, reteaching the activities in *Brain Awakes* serves as a reminder to your children to continue reaching for their highest potential.

"Students begin to develop the ability to regulate their stress and emotions, and pay more attention to their mind and body, not because a teacher or textbook instructs them to do so, but because yoga-based physical movement, breathing exercises, meditation practices and relaxation techniques provide them with an embodied and experiential sense of what it feels like to cultivate these skills."[3]

Thank you for your dedication to helping your children grow in their ability to recognize and regulate their emotions. Please reach out to share your stories, experiences, and questions involving *@BrainAwakes* by connecting with our community of empowerment on Facebook, Twitter, and Instagram.

About the Author

Joseph Hamer

Inspiring children to become aware of their greatest potential is why Joseph chose the path of an educator. Just seventeen days after graduating with honors from Emporia State University, he began his teaching career. Since then, Joseph has taught the first, second, and third grade in Wichita, Kansas. Mr. Hamer is known by his colleagues for creating a safe and uplifting environment for his students to continuously learn and grow. The Assistant Superintendent of all elementary schools in USD 259 recognized Joseph for his hard work and dedication to his students. After beginning his own journey of awareness in 2017, Joseph started teaching his students how to monitor and manage their emotions using mindfulness. The activities made such an incredible impact on his classroom community each year that he knew he needed to develop a tool for teachers and parents to replicate the results. Thus, the manifestation of *Brain Awakes*—a journey to empowerment.

About the Author

Hayley Peter

After noticing the need for fidget spinners, brain breaks, and flexible seating to encourage self-regulation: Hayley sought to understand a better way. She completed the certification to become a yoga instructor while receiving her Bachelor's in Education. The combination of mindfulness in the elementary classroom and education in the yoga studio, created a playground for Hayley to answer a big question: "What is the correlation between emotional awareness and one's ability to learn?" She sought to answer that question by empowering children with the tools they have within themselves, and to cultivate a sense of self-awareness and leadership. Hayley moved to California to experiment with different audiences and demographics. She wondered if cultivating a space of joy would help the learning process. While involving children in self inquiry and inquiry about social environments, she began to see children form connections with each other, various topics, and the world around them. With her colleague Joseph, Haley continues to be devoted to sharing many tools that serve in the adventure of lifelong learning.

About the Illustrator

Allison Stucky

Though *Brain Awakes* is the first book she has illustrated, Allison Stucky's art roots run deep. A proud Kansas native, Allison earned a BA in Art Education from Wichita State in 1996, and a Master of Arts in Teaching degree from Saint Mary's College in 2003. She has been teaching K—12 Art for the past 22 years in both rural and urban districts in Kansas. Currently teaching at Riverside Leadership Magnet Elementary School in Wichita, Allison was the runner-up for USD #259 Specials Distinguished Teacher Award in 2019. Along with teaching, she has showcased her art work in a variety of exhibitions in Kansas City and Wichita. Allison believes that through art, children have the outlet to find their unique voice, develop problem solving skills, and experience autonomy. Allison lives in Colwich, Kansas with her wife and six children.

References

[1] Laird, B. D., & Mester, E. (2018). Social and Emotional Learning in Elementary School. In J. Logan (Ed.), *Social and Emotional Learning in Out-of-School Time* (pp. 53-71). Charlotte, NC: Information Age Publishing.

[2] Himmelstein, D. (2019). Teaching with Heart: How Social-Emotional Learning Transforms Students and Schools. *School Library Journal*, 26–33.

[3] Butzer, B., Bury, D., Telles, S., & Khalsa, S. B. S. (2016). Implementing yoga within the school curriculum: a scientific rationale for improving social-emotional learning and positive student outcomes. *Journal of Children's Services*, *11*(1), 3–24. https://doi.org /10.1108/jcs-10-2014-0044

[4] Lerner, J. B. (2018). How Out-of-School Time Can Support College and Career Readiness Through Social and Emotional Learning. In C. Deeds (Ed.), *Social and Emotional Learning in Out-of-School Time* (pp. 125–144). essay, Information Age Publishing.

Made in the USA
Coppell, TX
10 July 2020

30424015R00066